Want to know
a lot to do

The Bicycle

Clavis

NEW YORK

Written by Lucas Arnoldussen
Illustrated by Mark Janssen

Ding-ding. Lisa rings the bell
as she gets on her bicycle.
She's going to ride home from school.

Do you ride your bike to school?
You probably love riding your bicycle,
but how much do you know about bicycles?

In this book you will learn all about bicycles.
So, grab your bike and come along for the ride!

Did you know

that the word *bicycle* is derived from the Latin word *bi*, which means "two," and the ancient Greek word *kúklos*, which means "circle" or "wheel"? So *bicycle* simply means "two wheels."

Dandy-horse or pedestrian bike

Dandy-horse with handlebars

Old-fashioned bicycles

People used to travel by **horse-drawn coach** or by boat. It was faster than walking, but was expensive. They started thinking about ways to get around that were less expensive.

Then someone in Germany invented the **draisine**, also called a pedestrian bicycle: two wheels made of wood with a wooden beam between them. You sat on the beam and pushed off from the ground with your feet. You clutched a handlebar with your hands, but you couldn't steer because the handlebar didn't move. You could go only straight ahead.

Later, someone invented a **draisine** with a handlebar that could turn. Now you could go around a corner.

Velocipede

High wheeler

A bicycle with pedals was first invented by two men in France. They called it a **vélocipède**. That means "quick feet." The wheels were made of iron, and pedals were attached to the front wheel.

They found out you could go faster if the front wheel was bigger than the rear wheel. So a bike was invented that was called **"the high bi."** By pedaling just a little, you moved forward very quickly. But it was not a very comfortable bike. Getting on it was quite difficult, and a fall could be dangerous since the seat was so high.

Mount your bike!

Today there are many different kinds of bicycles.
How many of these bikes do you recognize?

Men's bike frame

Recumbent bike

Tricycle

Delivery bike

BMX race bike

Balance bike

Women's bike frame

Cargo bike

Children's bicycle

Did you know electric bikes (also called ebikes) have a little motor to help riders get up hills.

Electric bicycle

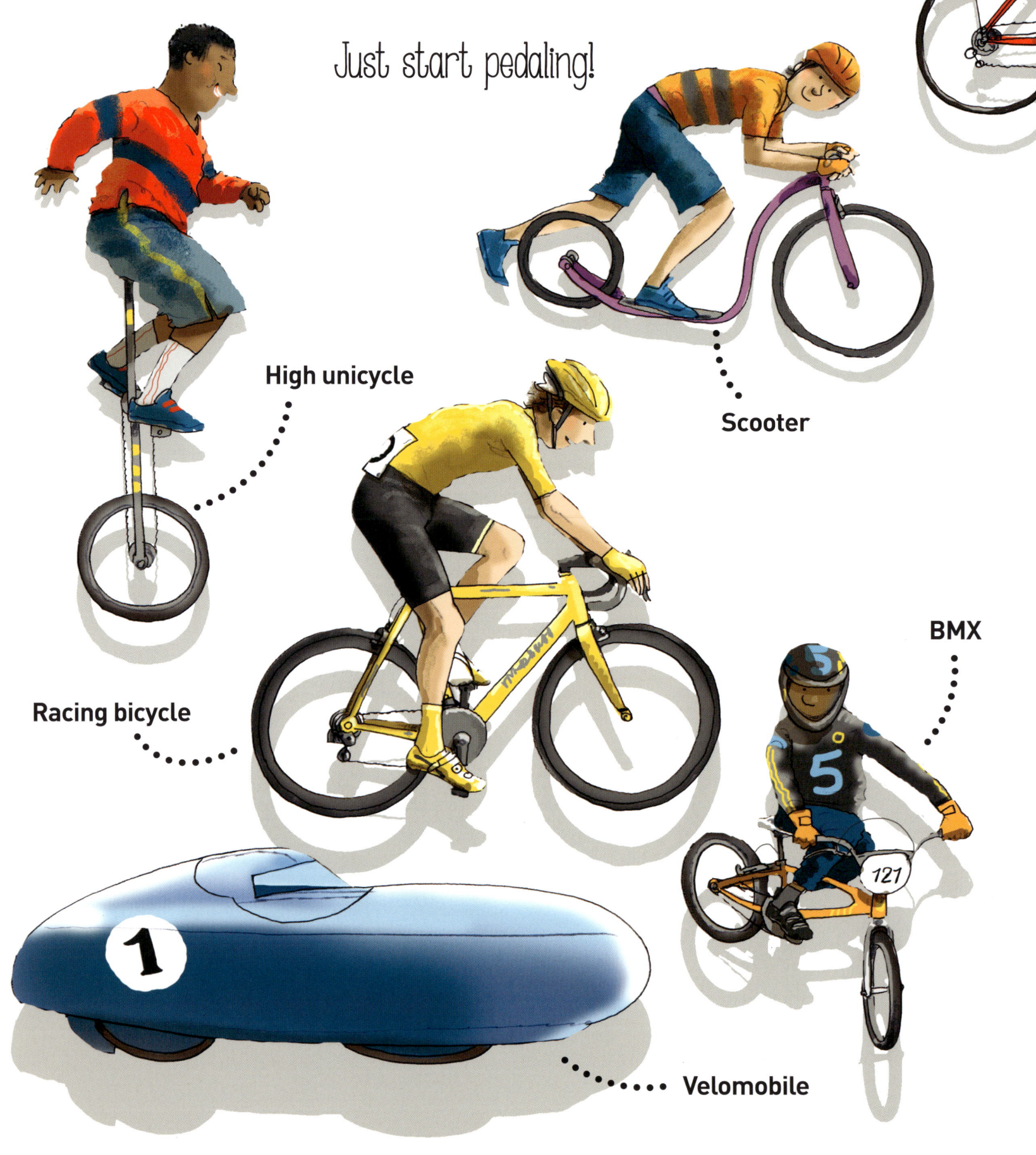

Just start pedaling!

High unicycle

Scooter

Racing bicycle

BMX

Velomobile

Recumbent tricycle

Tandem

Did you know
the longest tandem bike ever
built had 35 seats and was about
67 feet long!

Mountain bike

Unicycle

A modern bicycle

Bicycles have changed a lot over the years.
Modern bicycles have many features for safety and comfort.
Let's take a look!

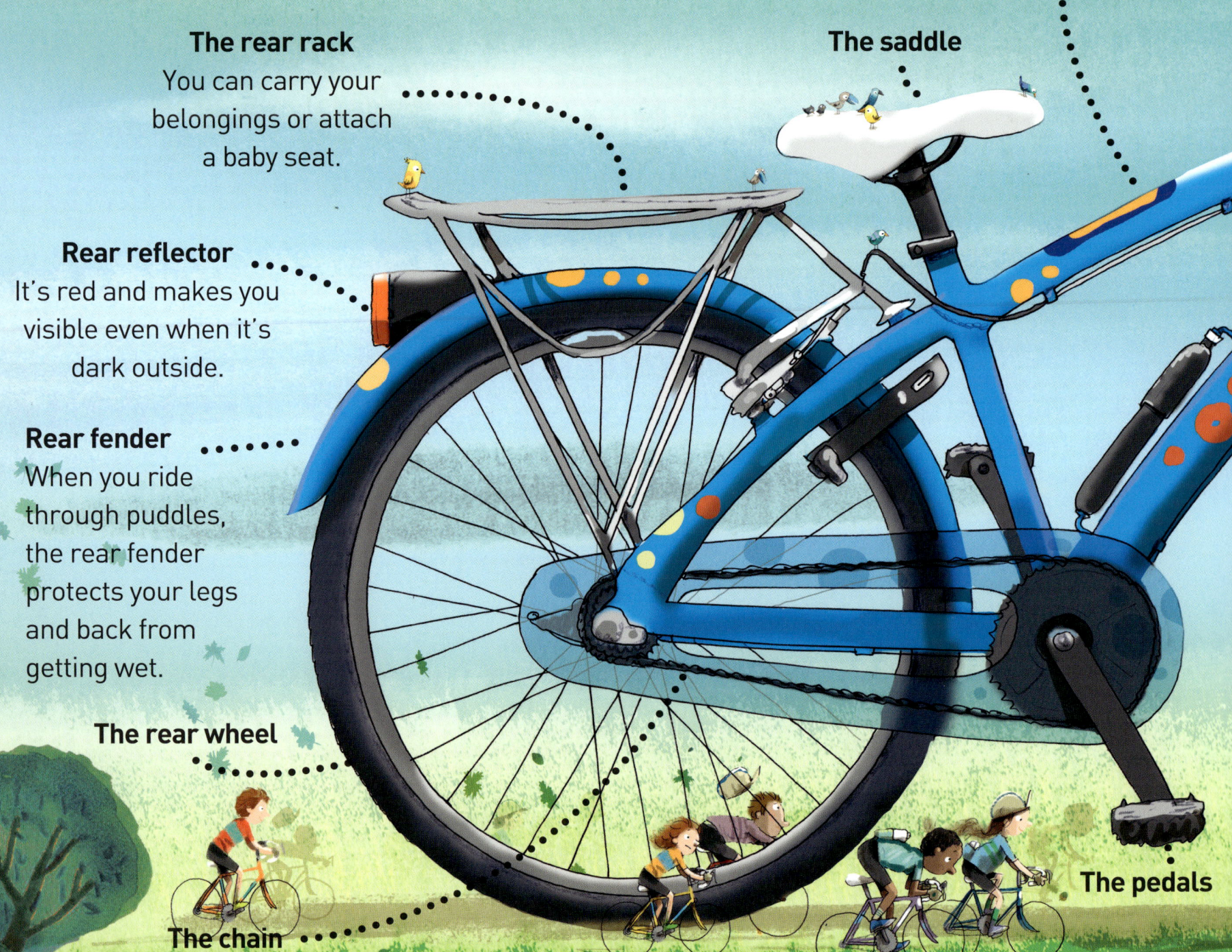

The frame
Wheels and pedals are
attached to the frame.

The rear rack
You can carry your
belongings or attach
a baby seat.

The saddle

Rear reflector
It's red and makes you
visible even when it's
dark outside.

Rear fender
When you ride
through puddles,
the rear fender
protects your legs
and back from
getting wet.

The rear wheel

The pedals

The chain
The chain makes it easier to pedal.

The bike bell
For warning other people that you are heading toward them.

The handlebars

Brakes
The brake on the handlebars is called a *handbrake*. Some bikes also have a *back-pedaling brake*, or a *coaster brake*.

The headlight
Its light is white. You switch it on as soon as it gets dark outside.

The pneumatic bike tire

Tire valve
Here is where you attach a pump to put air into the tire.

The spokes
To make the wheel stronger, but not too heavy.

The front wheel

Did you know the first bicycle did not have air-filled tires? Riders could feel every bump in the road. That is why in England they called the bike a **boneshaker**.

Doing your job on a bicycle

You probably use your bike to go from one place to another or just for fun.
But there are people who also use their bike every day at work.

Bicycle messengers or bike couriers

"I am a bicycle messenger. I deliver important packages around town. I am using a racing bicycle so I can go really fast. The packages are in a large backpack. Most of the time, I get to my destination faster than a car!"

The mail carrier

"I am a mail carrier. I deliver letters by bike. Sometimes a bike is more practical than a car, because I can park it anywhere. My bike has to be sturdy, to carry heavy bags filled with letters and packages."

The baker

"I work at a bakery. I deliver cakes and cookies with a delivery bike. I always ride my bike carefully, because I don't want the icing to drop off the cakes!"

The police officer

"I am a police officer. I use a bicycle to get around rather than a police car. I can go anywhere by bike, even in very narrow streets. And I can even chase somebody if necessary."

The ice cream vendor

"In the summer, I ride my ice cream bike to a park. Then I start selling ice cream. People love to come and buy a delicious treat."

The newspaper deliverer

"Every day, I deliver newspapers around my neighborhood. I have large bags to carry all the newspapers. When I get to a house, I stop and toss the paper to the front door."

Did you know

that biking is better for the environment than driving a car? And it's good for your health, too! Maybe we should all be using a bike more often!

Outer tube

Wrench

A spoke tensioner

A socket wrench

Chain oil

A racing bicycle

Tires

Inner tube

Air pump

Used bicycle

Choosing a bicycle

If you want to buy a bicycle, you can go to a bike shop. Bikes come in lots of different styles and sizes. That is why you can usually try out the bike before you buy it. You know if the size is right when you can touch the floor with both your feet while sitting on the saddle. What kind of brakes would you prefer? A hand brake or a back-pedaling brake? When you have chosen the right bike, you check to see whether it has everything you need. Headlight and reflectors? Does it have a bell?

Do you need to buy a lock? Is there a rear rack
with elastic straps? Or a flag on a pole so you are
more visible to cars? Fold out the pages and enter
the bike shop! There are a lot of bicycles lined up
here. Which one would you choose?

Children's bikes

Flags

New bicycles

Helmet

Lock

Spoke beads

Cash register

Bicycle bells

Many bike stores have a **service department**. They make sure your new bicycle is ready for you to ride. They also repair bikes that are broken.

Bike sports

There are many different sports that require a bicycle. Which one do you like most?

Mountain biking

In a mountain bike race, you don't ride on a road but in the woods. You cross mountains and hills and even water! Mountain bikes have thick, sturdy tires so they can tackle all kinds of terrain.

BMX

In a BMX race, you bike on a small, sandy circuit. A race takes only a few minutes! In the circuit there are high hills, so bike racers make spectacular jumps.

Did you know that

the most famous bicycle race is the Tour de France? It takes place in France every year during the summer. There are racers from all over the world.

Road racing

The one who crosses the finish line first wins. Some races are short distances and some are very long. Some even go on for many days. Racing bikes have really thin tires that make you go very fast, but they make it easier to fall down, too.

Freestyle BMX

A freestyle BMX contest is not about who passes the finish line first, but who can do the best tricks on a bike.

Spinning

Riding a stationary is called spinning. You can bike on a spinner or home trainer at the gym or at home. You can stay fit and you don't have to go outside when it's rainy or windy.

Famous cyclists

Road racing is a popular sport.
Some racers have become very famous.

1 Lucien van Impe

Lucien van Impe was a cyclist who was very good at going up mountains. He won most of his races that involved climbing high mountains. Lucien van Impe was the last Belgian racer to win the Tour de France.

2 Mario Cipollini

Mario Cipollini was an Italian sprinter. That means that he could bike the last bit of the race very fast. In a lot of contests the cyclists ride together in a group and then one of them dashes forward at the last moment.

3 Eddy Merckx

Eddy Merckx from Belgium was perhaps the best cyclist ever. He won 525 races! Nowadays, he often shows up on television to talk about cycling.

4 Lance Armstrong

Lance Armstrong was an American cyclist. After he had been severely ill, he won the Tour de France seven times in a row! Years later it appeared that Lance Armstrong had cheated. By using banned drugs, he had been able to cycle faster. He had to return all the medals he had won.

5 Joop Zoetemelk

The best Dutch cyclist until now is Joop Zoetemelk. His nickname was "he who always came in second," because he finished just after the winner six times at the Tour de France. But one time he succeeded at being first.

Tour de France 1976 Lucien!

Tour de France 1999 Mario!

Tour de France 1986 Joop!

Tour de France 1972 Eddy!

Tour de France 2001 Lance!

Look at all the kids on bicycles!

How many red helmets do you see?

How many blue helmets?

How many white helmets?

Can you find the tricycle?

Can you find the balance bike?

Which bike is carrying a ball?

How many bikes have flags?

Who is doing something dangerous?

Where do you think everyone is going?

How to fix a flat tire

This is what you need:

A bucket or tray filled with water

Tire levers

Sandpaper

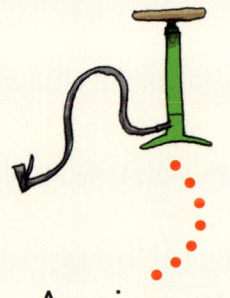
Tire patches

An air pump

Tire glue

Here is what you do:

1. Take off the outer tube with the tire levers.

2. Pump up the inner tube so you can find the leak.

3. Put the inner tube in the bucket of water. Look for small bubbles—that will tell you where the leak is.

4. With the sandpaper, rub the tire around the leak. This will make the glue stick better.

5. Smear the glue around the leak.

6. Stick a tire patch firmly onto the leak.

7. Pump up the inner tube again and put the outer tube around the wheel.

Where is Lisa going on her bike?

Lisa feels like eating something yummy. If you follow the direction of these arrows, you can find out where she is heading:

↑ ← ↑ → ↑ → ↑ → ↑ ← ↓

Vroom!

Using two clothes pins, attach a piece of cardboard or a playing card to the frame next to the front wheel. The card should stick out between the spokes. When you ride your bicycle, it will sound like . . . VROOM . . . a real motorbike!

Answers

1. Quick feet.

2. To make sure your legs don't get dirty when there is a puddle.

3. To alert people you are heading toward them.

4. Because he has to carry heavy bags.

5. Whether the frame is the right size for you.

6. Locks, bells, spoke beads, tires and tubes.

7. Mountain biking.

8. Cycling uphill.

9. Eddy Merckx.

10. Tire levers, a pump, a bucket or tray of water, sandpaper, tire glue, tire patches.

Mini-quiz

1. What does the word *velocipede* mean?

2. Why do bikes have a rear fender?

3. Why does a bike have a bell?

4. Why does a mail carrier need a sturdy bike?

5. What do you have check first when you go and buy a bike?

6. Can you list three things that you can buy in a bike shop?

7. In which bike sport do you ride in the woods?

8. What was the strength of cyclist Lucien van Impe?

9. Who was perhaps the best cyclist ever?

10. What do you need when repairing a flat tire?